Time to Celebrate!

LET'S GO TO A
PARADE!

By Benjamin Proudfit

Gareth Stevens
PUBLISHING

Please visit our website, www.garethstevens.com. For a free color catalog of all our high-quality books, call toll free 1-800-542-2595 or fax 1-877-542-2596.

Library of Congress Cataloging-in-Publication Data

Names: Proudfit, Benjamin, author.
Title: Let's go to a parade! / Benjamin Proudfit.
Description: New York : Gareth Stevens Publishing, 2020. | Series: Time to
  celebrate! | Includes index.
Identifiers: LCCN 2018044080| ISBN 9781538238981 (pbk.) | ISBN 9781538239001
  (library bound) | ISBN 9781538238998 (6 pack)
Subjects: LCSH: Parades–Juvenile literature.
Classification: LCC GT3980 .P76 2020 | DDC 394/.5–dc23
LC record available at https://lccn.loc.gov/2018044080

First Edition

Published in 2020 by
Gareth Stevens Publishing
111 East 14th Street, Suite 349
New York, NY 10003

Copyright © 2020 Gareth Stevens Publishing

Editor: Kristen Nelson
Designer: Katelyn E. Reynolds

Photo credits: Cover, p. 1 Blend Images - KidStock/Brand X Pictures/Getty Images; p. 5 Manny DaCunha/
Shutterstock.com; p. 7 Amy K. Mitchell/Shutterstock.com; pp. 9, 24 (police) Stuart Monk/Shutterstock.com; p. 11
Png Studio Photography/Shutterstock.com; p. 13 Richard Thornton/Shutterstock.com; pp. 15, 19 Roberto Galan/
Shutterstock.com; pp. 17, 24 (float) ksana05/Shutterstock.com; p. 21 Kobby Dagan/Shutterstock.com; p. 23 Jilll
Richardson/Shutterstock.com.

Printed in the United States of America

CPSIA compliance information: Batch #CS19GS: For further information contact Gareth Stevens, New York, New York at 1-800-542-2595.

Contents

We are going to a parade! Parades mark special days.

There are many people.
We all stand
along the street.

The police stand nearby.
They make sure
we are safe.

The mayor drives by.
He waves!

Bands march.
They play music.

They have many drums.

People in town
made floats!
Trucks pull them.

Amira rides
on a flower float.

We see dancers
in the parade.

What will your parade be like?

23

Words to Know

float

police

Index